Growing Together

K.L WHITE

Dedication
To the best daughter in the world

One sunny day at the School of Smiles, Mrs Lee announced an exciting new project: they were going to grow their own fruits and vegetables! Delcie, who loved plants, couldn't wait to get started.

“Today, we’re going to learn how to
grow our own food!” Mrs Lee said,
her smile brightening the room.

“Growing fruits and vegetables is not only fun,
but it also helps us understand where our food
comes from.”

Delcie raised her hand eagerly. "Can we plant something we can eat?"

"Absolutely!" Mrs Lee replied. "Let's start with some easy-to-grow plants for our UK climate. We'll go through step-by-step instructions for each one!"

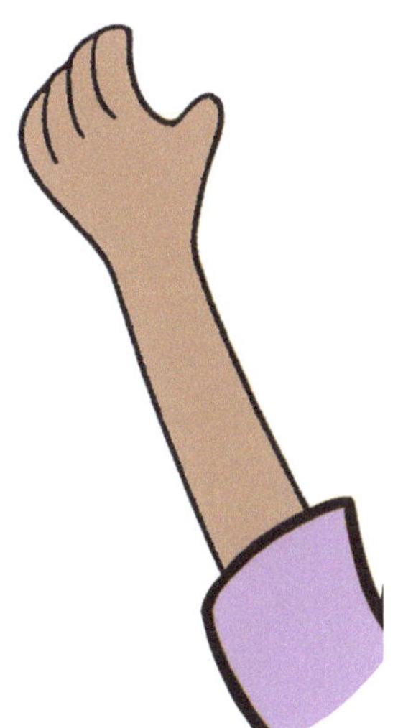

Before planting, Mrs Lee took the class outside to the school garden, where they could dig and prepare the soil.

"First, we need to prepare the soil," she said. "Let's turn it over and remove any weeds or stones. This helps our plants grow strong!"

Delcie picked up a shovel and got to work.

1. Gather tools: shovels, rakes, and gloves.

2. Clear the area: Remove weeds and stones from the garden bed.

3. Loosen the soil: Use a shovel to turn the soil, making it fluffy and easy to work with.

4. Add compost: Mix in some compost to enrich the soil. Delcie helped spread compost evenly across the garden.

YOU HAVE
TO WEAR
GLOVES
TO PROTECT
YOUR HANDS!

"Let's start with strawberries!" Mrs Lee said. "They're delicious and easy to grow."

Delcie smiled. Strawberries were her favourite fruit.

Instructions:

1. Choose a sunny spot: Strawberries need plenty of sunlight.

2. Prepare the soil: Ensure it's well-drained and mix in compost.

3. Plant the seeds: Space the seeds about 12 inches apart.Delcie planted her seeds carefully.

4. Water gently: After planting, give them a good drink but don't drown them.

5. Mulch: Add straw around the plants to keep moisture in and prevent weeds. Delcie spread the straw like a pro.

"Next, we'll grow carrots!" Mrs. Lee announced.
Delcie imagined pulling up long, crunchy carrots
from the soil.

Instructions

1. Choose a deep bed: Carrots need loose soil to grow long and straight.

2. Prepare the soil: Remove stones and weeds, then rake it smooth.

3. Sow the seeds: Create shallow rows and sprinkle the seeds about 2 inches apart.

4. Cover lightly: Sprinkle a thin layer of soil over the seeds.

5. Water carefully: Keep the soil moist until they sprout, usually in 2-3 weeks.

Delcie checked her row daily.

"Now, let's grow tomatoes!" Mrs Lee said. "These need a little extra care."

Delcie was curious—tomatoes were new to her.

Instructions:

1. Choose a sunny spot: Tomatoes love the sun!

2. Start seeds indoors: Plant seeds in pots about 6-8 weeks before the last frost.

3. Transplant outdoors: Once the seedlings are about 6 inches tall and the danger of frost has passed, plant them outside, 18 inches apart.

4. Support the plants: Use stakes (sturdy poles often made of wood or bamboo) or cages (like little wire towers that go around a plant to hold it up as it grows. They help the plant stay strong and keep its branches from falling over or breaking.) to support them as they grow.

5. Water regularly: Keep the soil moist but not soggy, especially during dry spells.

Over the next few weeks, Mrs Lee taught the class how to care for their plants. Delcie loved checking on them every day.

caring for the plants

1. Watering: Check the soil regularly. Water early in the morning or late in the evening.

2. Weeding: Remove any weeds that compete with their plants for nutrients. Delcie's careful hands made sure no weeds grew near her strawberries.

3. Pest control: Look for signs of pests, and if found, use natural remedies like soapy water. Delcie sprayed soapy water to protect the plants.

After weeks of care, the day finally came when they could harvest their fruits and vegetables. Mrs Lee gathered everyone around the garden.

Delcie spotted bright red strawberries. "Look! They're ready!" she shouted, rushing over to pick them.

Ayesha picked tomatoes, while Uche and Mats harvested carrots. Everyone cheered as they gathered their crops.

That Friday, Mrs Lee organized a garden feast. Each student brought something made with their homegrown produce.

Delcie brought strawberry muffins that she baked with her dad.

"These are my favourite recipe!" she announced proudly.

The classroom was filled with delicious smells. Mrs Lee smiled. "Thanks to our hard work, we have a beautiful meal to share!"

After the feast, Mrs Lee asked, "What did you learn from this experience?"

Delcie raised her hand.

"I learned that growing food is fun and teaches us patience. Plus, it's amazing to eat something you grew yourself!" she said with a big smile.

As the school year continued, Delcie and her friends visited the garden often, planting new crops and dreaming of new recipes.

They realized that, just like their diverse cultures, their garden was a mix of beautiful flavors and experiences.

Delcie looked at the thriving garden and smiled. She couldn't wait for the next adventure at the School of Smiles.

Gardening Tips

Here are some simple tips to help you start your very own garden:

1. Choose the Right Spot: Find a place that gets plenty of sunlight (most plants need 6-8 hours a day). Make sure it's easy to access for watering and care.

2. Start Small: Begin with a few easy-to-grow plants like strawberries, carrots, or tomatoes. You can also try growing herbs like basil, mint, or parsley in small pots.

3. Use Good Soil: Healthy plants start with good soil. Use compost or nutrient-rich soil to help your plants grow strong. If you don't have a garden, try planting in pots or containers with potting soil.

4. Water Wisely: Water your plants early in the morning or late in the evening when it's cooler. Don't overwater—keep the soil moist but not soggy.

5. Watch Out for Weeds: Weeds can steal nutrients from your plants. Pull them out regularly, especially after it rains.

6. Keep an Eye on Pests: Check your plants for bugs that might be eating the leaves or fruit. Use natural pest control, like soapy water, or ask an adult for help.

7. Be Patient: Plants take time to grow. Check them every day, but remember it may take weeks for them to sprout and produce fruit or vegetables.

8. Get Creative: Decorate your garden with painted rocks, signs, or wind chimes. Keep a gardening journal to draw pictures or write about your plants' progress.

9. Harvest Carefully: Wait until fruits and vegetables are ripe before picking them. Gently twist or cut them from the plant.

Share your harvest with family and friends—it tastes even better that way!

10. Have Fun!

Gardening is a great way to connect with nature. Celebrate your progress, even if not everything grows as planned. Every little effort helps you learn and grow!

Delcie Strawberry Muffin Recipe

(with adult supervision)

These strawberry muffins are soft, fruity, and made with wholesome ingredients—perfect for a healthy treat!

Ingredients (Makes 12 muffins)

1 ¾ cups (220g) whole wheat flour (or a mix of whole wheat and plain flour)

1 tsp baking powder

½ tsp baking soda

½ tsp salt

½ cup (120ml) honey or maple syrup

½ cup (120ml) plain yogurt (Greek or regular)

⅓ cup (80ml) olive oil or melted coconut oil

2 large egg

1 tsp vanilla extract

1 cup (150g) fresh strawberries, chopped

Instructions

Preheat the oven to 190°C (375°F) and line a muffin tin with paper liners or lightly grease it.

In a large bowl, whisk together the flour, baking powder, baking soda, and salt.

In another bowl, mix the honey (or maple syrup), yogurt, olive oil, eggs, and vanilla extract until smooth.

Add the wet ingredients to the dry ingredients and gently stir until just combined. Be careful not to overmix!

Fold in the chopped strawberries.

Spoon the batter evenly into the muffin tin, filling each cup about ¾ full.

Bake for 18–22 minutes, or until a toothpick inserted into the center of a muffin comes out clean.

Let the muffins cool in the tin for 5 minutes, then transfer them to a new surface to cool completely.

Enjoy these muffins as a snack, or a healthy dessert!